Che GUEVARA

DAVID DOWNING

Heinemann Library
Chicago, Illinois

Customer Service 888-454-2279

Visit our website at www.heinemannlibrary.com

Originated by Dot Gradations, Ltd.
Printed by South China Printing Company, Ltd.

07 06 05 04 03
10 9 8 7 6 5 4 3 2 1

Library of Congress Cataloging-in-Publication Data
Downing, David, 1946-
    Ernesto "Che" Guevara / David Downing.
        p. cm. -- (Leading lives)
Summary: Traces the life of the Latin American revolutionary and guerrilla fighter who joined Castro's movement to overthrow Cuba's government, served as minister of industry, and was killed while leading a Communist guerrilla force in Bolivia.
Includes bibliographical references and index.
    ISBN 1-40340-832-7 (Library binding)   1-4034-3493-X (pbk. bdg.)
    1. Guevara, Ernesto, 1928-1967--Juvenile literature. 2. Cuba--History--1959---Juvenile literature. 3. Latin America--History--1948-1980--Juvenile literature. 4. Guerrillas--Latin America--Biography--Juvenile literature. [1. Guevara, Ernesto, 1928-1967. 2. Guerrillas--Latin America. 3. Cuba--History--1959- 4. Latin America--History--1948-1980.] I. Title. II. Series.
    F2849.22.G85 D69 2003
    980.03'5'092--dc21

2002012399

Acknowledgments
The author and publishers are grateful to the following for permission to reproduce copyright material: pp. 4, 21, 23, 26, 32, 48, 51 Popperfoto; pp. 5, 17, 35 Rex Feature; pp. 6, 9, 11 Camera Press; p. 15 Jim Zuckerman/Corbis; pp. 18, 27, 29 Hulton Archive; pp. 22, 30, 33, 36 Bettman/Corbis; pp. 24, 25 Peter Newark's American Pictures; pp. 39, 40, 42 Corbis; p. 44 Perfecto Romero/CSC; p. 52 Rolando Pujol/South American Pictures; p. 54 Popperfoto/Reuters.

Cover photograph of Guevara reproduced with permission of Popperfoto.

Every effort has been made to contact copyright holders of any material reproduced in this book. Any omissions will be rectified in subsequent printings if notice is given to the publisher.

Some words are shown in bold, **like this.** You can find out what they mean by looking in the glossary.

Contents

1 Life After Death

In July 1997, in the middle of the South American winter, a small group of Cubans arrived in the Bolivian town of Vallegrande to begin the hunt for the body of their national hero. The Argentine-born Ernesto "Che" Guevara had fought in the Cuban **revolutionary** war some 40 years earlier. He also had been a leading figure in the government that grew out of the revolutionaries' victory. In 1967, he was killed during an attempt to start a new **revolution** in Bolivia. Until recently, people believed that his murderers had **cremated** his body. Now, however, new evidence suggested that the assassins had buried Guevara near Vallegrande's small airfield. After several weeks of searching, the Cubans unearthed the bodies of three men. One of them was identified as Guevara's.

The Cubans flew Guevara's body north to Cuba, where he had made his name as a **guerrilla** fighter and political leader. Cuba had launched him on his short but dazzling career as a revolutionary hero and turned him into something unique—a world-famous enemy of both the United States and the Soviet Union, of both international **capitalism** and international **Communism.**

◀ Che Guevara's body leaves the Cuban capital of Havana for burial on October 14, 1997. In the background a government building is adorned with the Cuban flag and an image of Guevara's face.

While most people supported either capitalism or Communism, Guevara had seemed aware of the flaws in both. Now, Cuba welcomed him back. More than 30 years after his death, hundreds of thousands of people lined up to pay their respects to the man in the flag-draped casket.

People remember Guevara all over the world. Images of his face are stencilled on the walls of buildings throughout **Latin America,** a continuing inspiration for all those who seek **radical** change and social justice. In the wealthier parts of the world—countries in Europe and North America, for example—the same face stares out from T-shirts, posters, books, and CD cases. In these countries, Guevara's face has become an image of youthful protest, of saying no to the way the older generation runs the world. But his face has become so familiar that at times it seems like nothing more than a fashion accessory, a badge of cool worn by people who have little idea about the man himself.

▲ *A multicolored drawing of Che Guevara stares fiercely from a Havana wall in 1993.*

So who was Ernesto "Che" Guevara and why is his memory still so precious to so many? How did an Argentinian with a serious lifelong illness end up fighting in the Cuban Revolution? How was it possible, at the height of the **Cold War** between the United States and the Soviet Union, for him to become an enemy to both countries? And what, in the end, took him from Cuba to that grave beside the airfield in the small Bolivian town of Vallegrande?

Childhood and Youth

Ernesto Guevara de la Serna, the future Che Guevara, was born on May 14, 1928, in the Argentine city of Rosario. He was the first child of Ernesto Guevara Lynch and Celia de la Serna y Llosa. During the next fifteen years, his parents would have four more children: Celia, Ana María, Roberto, and Juan Martín.

Ernesto Sr., whose family roots in Argentina stretched back many generations, could consider himself a member of the country's **nobility.** His wife Celia had inherited much money and property. Despite their wealth, people knew the family for its **socialist** opinions and its desire for a fairer society. Like

Celia, Ernesto Sr.'s mother Ana Lynch—the only grandmother that Guevara ever knew—actively campaigned for women's rights. Celia's sister, Carmen, and her poet husband Cayetano both belonged to the Argentine **Communist** Party.

A lifelong affliction

During the first years of Guevara's life, the family lived in San Isidro, close to the Argentine capital of Buenos Aires.

◀ *As a small boy, Ernesto Guevara de la Serna lived in San Isidro, Argentina.*

What is asthma?

Asthma is an illness that makes it difficult for a person to breathe. An asthma attack occurs when the muscles in the tubes that connect the throat with the lungs tighten. The muscles make the tubes narrower, so that it is hard for air to pass through them. A serious asthma attack makes it almost impossible for a person to breathe and can cause death. Infections, physical activity, and allergies can all trigger an attack or make an attack more severe. Asthma can be treated with drugs that lessen the symptoms.

There, a few days before his second birthday, Guevara had his first **asthma** attack. For three terrifying years, these attacks struck almost every day. Slowly but surely, medical care, the devotion of his parents, and Guevara's own efforts combined to ease the problem. But he would struggle with the disease for the rest of his life.

The early years of asthma attacks created a lifelong bond between Guevara and his mother. He spent many days lying in bed, and Celia would read and talk to him. She would encourage his curiosity about the world and stimulate his love of learning.

Guevara always had a balloon of oxygen with him to help him through his asthma attacks. However, according to his father, he would only use it at the last minute. "He did not want to depend on this treatment, and he tried to bear the attack as long as he could, but when he could no longer stand it and his face was turning purple from the choking, he would wriggle and point to his mouth to indicate that it was time. The oxygen relieved him immediately."

El Loco

Around 1935, the family moved to the hill town of Alta Gracia. The family hoped that the cleaner air there would be good for Guevara's illness. He attended school only occasionally at first, but with increasing regularity between the ages of ten and eleven. When he was too sick to go to school, he studied at home, determined to make up for what he was missing.

Encouraged by his father, Guevara was equally determined to succeed at sports and other physical activities. He was always eager to prove that his illness would not hold him back or limit him in any way. As a teenager his classmates nicknamed him *El Loco* (the crazy one) because of his recklessness. He jumped off high rocks into rivers, tightrope-walked his way across deep ravines, and rode his bike along railway tracks.

Despite his physical weakness, Guevara was clearly a natural leader from an early age. One fellow pupil later told how "the children followed him around a lot in the schoolyard; he would climb up a big tree that was there, and all the kids stood around him as if he were the leader, and when he ran the others followed behind him; it was clear that he was the boss."

Growing up

In 1936, when Guevara was eight years old, the **Spanish Civil War** broke out. Most Argentinians had Spanish roots, and they followed reports of the conflict with great interest. This was particularly true of the Guevara household. Guevara's Uncle Cayetano went to Spain as a newspaper reporter, and his family came to live with the Guevaras. This meant that Guevara was able to follow the progress of the war closely. He hung a huge map of Spain on his bedroom wall and tried to create a small-scale battlefield in the backyard. In 1943 the family moved some 25 miles (40 kilometers) to the

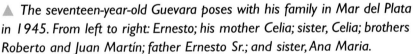 *The seventeen-year-old Guevara poses with his family in Mar del Plata in 1945. From left to right: Ernesto; his mother Celia; sister, Celia; brothers Roberto and Juan Martín; father Ernesto Sr.; and sister, Ana Maria.*

much larger city of Córdoba, where Guevara was already attending high school. He was only an average student, doing well in those subjects that interested him, such as literature and **philosophy,** and not so well in those that did not, such as music and physics. He swam, played tennis and golf, and grew to love chess. He also enjoyed the challenge of playing rugby. If, as often happened, he suffered an asthma attack during a game, he would leave the field to give himself an injection of **adrenaline.**

Student

In 1946, Guevara finished high school and took a part-time job with the local roads department. His family was in the process of moving to Buenos Aires, but the eighteen-year-old Guevara wanted to stay in Córdoba to study engineering at the local university. He may have wanted to stay near his friends, or he may have been eager to leave the family home. His parents had begun to fight bitterly over money and a range of other family issues.

In Buenos Aires, Guevara's grandmother became seriously sick, and Celia needed her son's help in caring for her during her final months. Celia had herself recently undergone surgery for cancer, and it seems likely that his mother's illness, his grandmother's impending death, and his own long struggle with asthma combined to convince Guevara to study medicine instead of engineering. In 1947, he registered at the Faculty of Medicine in Buenos Aires and spent the next four years as a medical student, specializing in the treatment of **allergies.**

Guevara's life became that of a hardworking, hard-playing student. He never cared about his appearance. He never combed his hair or tied his shoelaces, and he went long periods without bathing. This earned him the nickname *El Chancho* (the pig). None of these habits seemed to affect his ability to date women. By 1950, he was involved with a woman named Chichina, whom he had met several years earlier in Córdoba.

His love of travel, however, more than matched his love for Chichina. During one summer vacation, he toured northern Argentina on a motorcycle, visiting his old Córdoba friend Alberto Granado at the **leper colony** where he worked.

In another vacation, he worked as a deck hand on a merchant ship, visiting Brazil, Trinidad, Venezuela, and the southern ports of Argentina.

Late in 1951, Granado told Guevara that he had taken a job at another leper colony in far-off Venezuela and suggested that they travel there together by motorcycle. Guevara said yes. His desire to see the world was stronger than either his love for Chichina or his commitment to his medical studies.

▼ *Guevara traveled throughout Argentina in his student days.*

3 Motorcycle Odyssey

Guevara and Granado set off on their trip to Venezuela in January 1952, at the height of the South American summer. But they soon ran into difficulties. Granado's motorcycle, which he called *La Poderosa* (the powerful one), broke down often on the unpaved roads. Also, the two men were thrown off their bikes again and again—nine times on one particularly bad day. Off the road, they added to their own problems by careless behavior. Once, they climbed a mountain and lingered there too late to get down before nightfall.

Another night, while staying with a farmer, they heard that a **puma** was prowling in the area. Guevara panicked when he saw two eyes glowing in the dark. He fired a revolver in their direction, only to discover that he had shot the farmer's dog. Things went from bad to worse when, a few days later, he picked up a forwarded letter from Chichina telling him that their relationship was over.

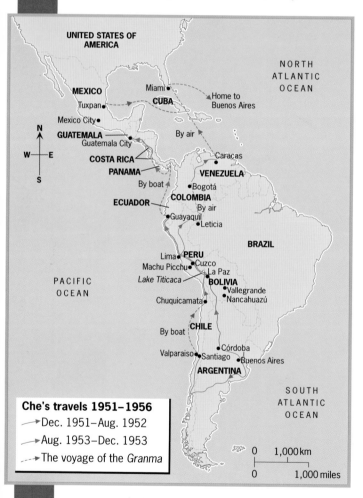

Che's travels 1951–1956
→ Dec. 1951–Aug. 1952
→ Aug. 1953–Dec. 1953
---→ The voyage of the *Granma*

0   1,000 km
0   1,000 miles

▲ This map shows Guevara's route through South and Central America between the years of 1951 and 1956.

Guevara and Granado's adventures continued in Chile. *La Poderosa* was

Latin America

Latin America is the name usually given to those parts of the Americas that Spain and Portugal conquered in the 1400s and 1500s and where the people speak Spanish or Portuguese. Latin America includes all of Central America, the Spanish-speaking islands of the Caribbean, and almost all of continental South America. The populations include the descendants of those **indigenous** people conquered by the European **colonial** powers, the descendants of slaves brought from Africa, European **immigrants,** and people of mixed race.

Traditionally, Europe and North America used Latin America as a source of minerals, food products, and other raw materials. In each country, small groups controlled the production of these raw materials. These small groups of rich and powerful local people, or **elites,** grew richer, but the wider population remained poor. By the time of Guevara's birth, almost all Latin American countries were politically independent of their former colonial masters. However, North American and European businesses, working in combination with the elites, largely controlled Latin American economies. The vast majority of ordinary people remained caught up in lifelong struggles to feed, clothe, and house themselves.

falling to pieces, and it finally collapsed altogether on one steep Chilean hill. Guevara and Granado managed to convince a truck driver to give them a ride to the Chilean capital of Santiago, but *La Poderosa* was beyond repair. For the rest of their journey, the two travelers had to depend on transportation from others.

The shadow of injustice

In the Chilean port of Valparaíso, Guevara agreed to visit a friend of the person with whom they were staying. The friend was an elderly and poverty-stricken woman who, like Guevara, suffered from **asthma.** The conditions in which she lived horrified him. "The poor thing was in an awful state," he wrote. "It is in cases like this, when a doctor knows he is powerless . . . that he longs for change, a change which would prevent the injustice of a system in which . . . this poor old woman had had to earn her living as a waitress, wheezing and panting."

Heading north

In Valparaíso, Guevara and Granado sneaked on board a ship heading north, coming out of hiding only when the ship was at sea. Getting off the ship in northern Chile, they crossed the desert to visit the huge copper mine at Chuquicamata. Then they journeyed north. For the next two months they traveled through the mountains of Peru, often riding in the backs of trucks with groups of **Andeans.** These people and their culture fascinated Guevara. They also visited the remains of the **Inca** civilization, the ruins of which are located on the shores of Lake Titicaca, in the old Inca capital of Cuzco, and in the Inca city of Machu Picchu. These ruins enormously impressed Guevara.

FOR A MAP OF GUEVARA'S TRAVELS, SEE PAGE 12.

The two men were often cold and hungry in the mountains. To get food, they would perform their anniversary routine, casually telling strangers that they set out on their trip exactly a year ago. How sad, they would add, that they did not have the money to celebrate. The strangers would usually buy them a drink, which they would happily accept. When offered a second drink, Guevara, however, would reluctantly refuse.

▲ *Guevara visited the ruins of the Inca city of Machu Picchu on both his journeys through South America.*

When asked why, he would explain that in Argentina it was the custom to eat and drink at the same time. The strangers would then buy them food. According to Guevara, this trick never failed to get them a meal.

Amazonia

From the Peruvian capital of Lima, Guevara and Granado headed back across the Andes and down into the upper reaches of the **Amazon basin.** Guevara had suffered many asthma attacks in the thin air of the mountains, but down in the tropical lowlands they grew more frequent and more severe. As they traveled down the Ucayali River, Guevara spent most of his time lying in a hammock, cursing the mosquitoes and, as he wrote in his diary, staring "dreamily out at the tempting jungle beyond the riverbank."

Their destination now was the San Pablo **leper colony,** which they reached on June 8. They stayed for twelve days, helping out where they could and proving highly popular with the residents. "Their appreciation," Ernesto wrote, "stemmed from the fact that we did not wear overalls or gloves, that we shook hands with them as we would the next man, sat with them, chatting about this and that, and played football with them. This may seem pointless bravado, but the psychological benefit to these poor people—usually treated like animals—of being treated as normal human beings is incalculable and the risk [of catching leprosy] incredibly remote."

Leprosy

Leprosy is a disease of the skin and nerve-endings that causes loss of feeling in the skin and nerves and organ and tissue damage. Weakness in the fingers and toes may cause them to curl inward. Throughout history, people have feared leprosy. Until recently, most people treated those suffering from the disease, called lepers, as outcasts. Medical officials virtually imprisoned lepers in out-of-the-way camps called leper colonies. In recent years, this situation has changed for the better, as more and more people have become aware that leprosy is not highly contagious.

Journey's end?

From San Pablo, Guevara and Granado rafted down the river to the Colombian port of Leticia, caught a plane to Bogotá, and then took buses to the Venezuelan capital of Caracas. There, after almost seven months together on the road, the two men parted company. Granado headed off to his job in

▶ *Guevara (right) and Granado rafted down the Amazon River in 1952.*

the leper colony, and Guevara caught a ride on an Argentinian plane transporting horses to Miami. The plane was supposed to spend only one day on the ground in the United States before returning to Argentina, but the pilots discovered a serious problem in one of the engines. Without any money, Guevara found himself stranded in Miami for a month. He stayed with a cousin of Chichina's and spent most of his time on the beach.

He finally reached home on August 31, 1952. He had promised his mother that he would finish his medical studies. He threw himself into his studies, passing fourteen exams in only a few months. He became a doctor in July 1953. However, medicine no longer interested him. His trip with Granado had opened his eyes to the enormous gap between rich and poor in South America. He realized that medicine could achieve little in such a situation. People who lacked food, clothing, and shelter, and who often worked long hours in dirty and dangerous conditions, would never be healthy. They needed a change in these conditions before they needed doctors.

The trip had also deepened Guevara's love of travel and his sense of adventure. He wanted more. Barely a month after qualifying as a doctor, Guevara was on the move again, heading north with another friend from his school days, Carlos "Calica" Ferrera. As their train pulled out of Retiro Station in Buenos Aires, Guevara's weeping mother ran alongside, convinced that she would never see her son again.

17

4 Guatemala and Fidel

Guevara and Ferrera first stopped in Bolivia. A **revolution** had taken place there in April 1952, and Guevara was eager to see how things had changed. But the results disappointed him. The state had taken over the mines that supplied much of the country's wealth, and the government initiated only limited **land reforms.** The gap between rich and poor, powerful and powerless, had not closed. A few families still owned most of the fertile land, leaving the vast majority with either no land at all or small, rocky plots. Guevara saw U.S. supervisors treat **Andean** workers poorly and watched **peasants** being sprayed with insecticide as they lined up to see officials. This revolution, he decided, had not gone far enough.

▲ Bolivian peasants work on a terraced hillside in the Andes. The peasants' lives of poverty and abuse spurred Guevara on in his fight for social change.

FOR A MAP OF GUEVARA'S TRAVELS, SEE PAGE 12.

The two men traveled across Peru, eventually reaching the port of Guayaquil in southern Ecuador. There, they ran into a group of travelers on their way to Guatemala, where another

Guatemala

In 1944, after many years of **dictatorship,** Guatemala enjoyed its first free elections. Later, governments led by presidents Arevalo and Arbenz introduced health care systems in the cities and laws to protect workers from being overworked and underpaid on foreign-owned coffee and banana plantations. In 1952, Arbenz introduced a land reform plan that involved transferring land from the U.S.-owned company United Fruit to poor peasants. The government offered to pay for the land, but United Fruit and the U.S. government declared that the amount was not enough. The dispute was reaching its climax when Guevara arrived in Guatemala in December 1953.

revolution seemed to be taking place. The **democratically elected** government, led by President Jacob Arbenz, was challenging United Fruit, the U.S. company that dominated the Guatemalan economy. Unlike the Bolivians, Arbenz was the type of **revolutionary** that Guevara appreciated. Guevara decided that Venezuela and Ferrera could wait. Parting company with Ferrera, he set out for Guatemala.

In the middle of a revolution

It took Guevara two eventful months to reach Guatemala City. In Panama, he was published for the first time—two travel articles on the **Inca** settlement of Machu Picchu and Amazonia. In Costa Rica he met a Peruvian revolutionary named Hilda Gadea. She introduced Guevara to some Cuban revolutionaries. They told him about their leader, Fidel Castro, and how he had led an attack on the Cuban government's military barracks at Moncada the previous June. The Cubans called Guevara *Che,* the Argentinian word for *buddy*, often used by other Latin Americans when talking to Argentinians.

Guevara reached Guatemala in the final days of 1953 and would remain there until the following August. Unable to practice medicine because he was a foreigner, he sold encyclopedias and took on part-time work in a laboratory to earn a living. He also suffered frequent **asthma** attacks. Despite all this, the situation excited him. He could have made money if he wanted—all he needed to do, he told his mother in a letter, was open a clinic specializing in **allergies.** But that, he wrote, "would be the most horrible betrayal of the two 'I's struggling inside me: the **socialist** and the traveler." The socialist wanted to save the world, and the traveler wanted to see the world. Neither, however, had time to run a clinic.

For the moment, the socialist was in control. He studied the writings of famous socialists and **Communists** and discussed politics endlessly with other **revolutionaries.** Hilda Gadea, who had also traveled to Guatemala, had become a close friend. She helped him through bouts of illness and introduced him to many people.

Meanwhile, U.S. and Guatemalan business interests were concerned about the Guatemalan government's planned program of social and economic reforms. They designed the program to improve the conditions of ordinary Guatemalans, but business leaders feared that it would greatly reduce their profits. They tried to persuade the government to think again. When that failed, a U.S.-sponsored invasion was launched in June 1954, and Guatemala City was bombed. Guevara wrote that he "thoroughly enjoyed himself" during these days of crisis. But he also admitted to feeling a little ashamed of enjoying events in which violence killed many people. But the excitement did not last long. Instead of putting up a fight, as Guevara had hoped it would, the Arbenz government began

▶ *Guatemalan rebels gather in the town of Esquipilas during the U.S.-sponsored invasion of 1954. Guevara was disappointed that the Guatemalan government did not put up more of a fight against the invaders.*

to fall apart. Betrayed by its own army, the government refused to arm those who, like Guevara, were willing to take on the invaders. By the end of June, the government had been overthrown, and Guevara had become one of many revolutionaries who were forced to seek **asylum** in the Argentine embassy.

There, he had several weeks to think about what had gone wrong. He had no doubt that Arbenz had been right to take on the United States. Events had proved that the United States would never willingly allow a revolution that threatened U.S.-business profits in **Latin America.** But Guevara was equally certain that Arbenz should have created a revolutionary army for the protection of his revolutionary government. And he should not have allowed the opposition so much freedom, particularly in the press, to criticize his revolution, because that had weakened the resistance to U.S. pressure. When the time came in Cuba, Guevara would remember these lessons.

Ready for action

Guevara eventually moved on to Mexico. For a while, he made a living photographing U.S. tourists, before finding some part-time research work studying **allergies.** He had a nice apartment, ate well, and even took a bath every day. His friendship with Hilda turned into a romance.

FOR DETAILS ON KEY PEOPLE OF GUEVARA'S TIME, SEE PAGE 58.

However, his anger remained. He believed that the events he had witnessed in Guatemala had proved him right, and he wrote to his mother of his "growing indignation" at the way in which the *gringos* (white foreigners) treated Latin Americans. He was ready for action and ready for the opportunity to fight for what he had missed in Guatemala.

In the summer of 1955, Guevara met Fidel Castro. Castro was the leader of the failed assault on the Moncada barracks and of the Cuban July 26 Movement, named after the date on which the assault took place. The two men hit it off immediately. Guevara joined Castro on his seaborne assault on the Cuban government as the expedition's doctor.

▲ *The young guerrillas rest in the jungle. Guevara is second from left, and Castro stands in the center with his brother Raul kneeling in front of him.*

That same summer he married Hilda, who became pregnant. Their daughter Hildita was born in February 1956, but there was little possibility

22

Fidel Castro

Fidel Castro was nearing his 29th birthday when he first met Guevara in the summer of 1955. Born in Cuba's Oriente province, Castro had studied and practiced law in the early 1950s before deciding to concentrate on politics. When Fulgencio Batista seized power in 1952, destroying Cuban democracy and setting himself up as a dictator, Castro organized and led an assault on Santiago de Cuba's Moncada military barracks on July 26, 1953. The assault failed, and Castro received a long prison sentence. But the government released him as part of a general **amnesty** in the summer of 1955. Moving to Mexico, Castro went to work forming his July 26 Movement, which, less than four years later, would drive Batista from Cuba.

▶ *Hilda Gadea speaks in London in 1969, two years after Guevara's murder in captivity.*

that Guevara would settle down with this new family. He had already found another family that was more important to him, the family of **revolutionaries.**

Throughout 1956, the preparations for Castro's assault continued. In the Cuban **guerrillas'** training camp Guevara finally became known simply as Che. Despite his **asthma,** he regularly came in first in all the fitness and military training exercises. By the end of the year, he had repeatedly demonstrated that he was much more than just the expedition's doctor. When the boat that Castro had purchased, the *Granma,* finally sailed for Cuba in December 1956, Che Guevara, the only non-Cuban on board, was already one of Fidel Castro's most trusted people.

The journey to Cuba was supposed to take five days, but it took seven. There were 82 men on a boat that had room for only 20, and most of them became seasick. A faulty clutch slowed the craft down, and a storm washed half the supplies overboard. The *Granma* finally reached the Cuban coast two days late and landed at the wrong spot. The landing forced the small army to spend several hours cutting their way through a swamp before they finally reached dry land.

FOR A MAP OF GUEVARA'S TRAVELS, SEE PAGE 12.

A guide sent by local supporters betrayed the hungry, exhausted force. Three days after the landing, Batista's soldiers and planes suddenly attacked them in the sugarcane fields of Alegría del Pío. By the end of that day, the twenty or so survivors were stumbling through the night in the general direction of Cuba's highest mountains, the Sierra Maestra. The Cuban **Revolution** had gotten off to a bad start.

The first few weeks

A Cuban soldier had shot Che Guevara in the neck at Alegría del Pío. The amount of blood pouring from the wound convinced him that he was about to die. For a few seconds he just sat there, remembering how a character in a book he had read had calmly leaned back against a tree and died in a dignified manner. But one of his fellow **guerrillas** rudely interrupted him, shouting that he should get moving, and Guevara found that he was not dying after all. The wound was not as bad as it looked.

◀ *The army of the July 26 Movement overthrew the Cuban dictator Fulgencio Batista.*

▶ *A Cuban poster of the 1960s featured heroes of the revolution. Guevara—center column, second picture—is below Fidel Castro and above Camilo Cienfuegos.*

About two weeks later, Guevara's small group met up with the other surviving fighters—including Castro, his brother Raul, and the popular Camilo Cienfuegos—in the foothills of the mountains. In mid-January 1957, they attacked a small military post, capturing weapons and regaining the confidence they had lost in those disastrous first few days. Soon, new recruits and fresh supplies were flowing into the mountains from July 26 Movement supporters in Cuba's towns. More small **skirmishes** with the army followed. But already the local **peasants** were siding with the guerrillas, sharing their knowledge of the countryside and warning of army movements.

In late January, during a skirmish in a gorge called Hell's Ravine, Guevara killed one of Batista's soldiers with a rifle shot. It was the first time he had killed a person. A few weeks later, he ordered—and, according to some accounts, carried out—the execution of a fellow guerrilla, Eutimio, who had tried to betray the group to the authorities. In these first weeks of the **revolutionary** war, Guevara discovered that he could turn off his emotions and be utterly ruthless if he was convinced that the situation required it. In addition, despite repeated **asthma** attacks, he toured the local villages with his doctor's bag and any medicine that he had.

25

His own command

Guevara got along well with Castro. They respected each other and found that they could argue without creating any lasting problems. In May, with Guevara leading bravely from the front, the **guerrillas** successfully attacked a small military post at El Uvero. After this victory, Castro split his army, now 200 strong, into two columns, or groups, and appointed Guevara commander—*comandante*—of the 75-strong second column. According to Guevara, "the dose of vanity that we all have inside made me feel the proudest man on Earth."

Guevara and his men fought several successful **skirmishes** against Batista's army during that summer and fall. They also set up their own base at El Hombrito in the Sierra Maestra. It included a bread oven, a printing press, a simple hospital, and a weapons supply. Guevara also organized classes to teach his soldiers and the local villagers how to read and write.

FOR A MAP OF IMPORTANT CUBAN SITES, SEE PAGE 28.

A hard man to follow

Che was well-organized, clever, and courageous to the point of foolhardiness. After he was shot in the foot in December 1957, Castro scolded him for taking too many risks. He accepted no privileges of rank. On the contrary, he insisted on receiving exactly the same treatment as everyone else.

◄ *Guevara (in black hat) and his column captured the central Cuban town of Santa Clara in December 1958.*

He lined up for food like all the others and took the same portions. Such behavior won him the lifelong loyalty of many who fought with him, and several would later follow him to their death in Bolivia.

However, a darker side existed to Guevara's fierce insistence on shared discipline and equality. He was a bad man to cross. He was ruthless to traitors, and he refused to make allowances for others' weaknesses. He never asked anyone to do anything that he was not prepared to do himself, but he did insist that everyone else live up to his own high standards. Since few people possessed his courage, intelligence, or determination, most people disappointed him.

▶ *Castro and Guevara enjoy themselves in the Sierra Maestra of Cuba, early in the revolutionary war.*

Friendly encouragement

"We [Guevara and his fellow-guerrilla Crespo] had to move fast to reach the hillside and cross to the other side before the troops cut us off, but it was not difficult because we had seen them in time . . . Everybody made it to the top, but for me it was a terrible experience. I was practically choking by the time I reached the top of the hill. I remember Crespo's efforts to make me walk. Every time I said I could not go on and asked to be left behind, Crespo would revert to our jargon and snap at me: '. . . either you walk or I'll hit you with my rifle butt!' "

(Guevara, writing in *The Revolutionary War*, was suffering badly from asthma at the time of this skirmish)

The final push

In the early summer of 1958, Batista launched a great offensive against the revolutionaries in the Sierra Maestra, sending in 10,000 reluctant troops against the 300 or so **guerrillas.** It was a disaster. Batista's soldiers could not find the guerrillas, but every now and then the guerrillas found them. By August, the guerrillas had killed or wounded 1,000 of Batista's troops and taken another 400 prisoner. These events signaled the end for Batista's **dictatorship.**

▼ *This map of Cuba shows the locations where important events occurred during Guevara's involvement with the island.*

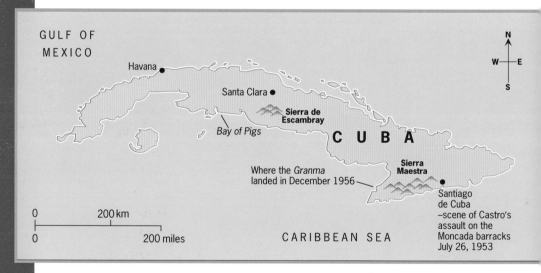

Castro decided the guerrillas should leave their mountain nests. That summer he ordered Guevara and Camilo Cienfuegos to lead two columns up the island to a new base in the Sierra de Escambray. It took 46 days for Guevara's 148 men to march the 180 miles (290 kilometers), battling mosquitoes, hurricanes, hunger, and the few members of Batista's army and air force that still had the will to fight.

Nevertheless, by mid-October the rebels had firmly established themselves in the center of the island, and Batista's control was fast slipping away. During this period, Guevara met a young woman named Aleida March, who was working as a **courier** between the rebel armies and their supporters in the towns. The sixth daughter of a local farmer, she would become his second wife in June of the following year, after his divorce from Hilda.

By late December, the town of Santa Clara was all that stood between Guevara and the open road to Cuba's capital of Havana. His men were outnumbered by at least ten to one, but Batista's soldiers had little interest in fighting.

Falling in love

Early in the battle for the town of Santa Clara, Aleida left Guevara's side to dash across a street that was under fire. For a few seconds she was out of sight, and he was not sure if she had made it safely. In those few seconds, he said later, he realized that he was in love with her.

They were counting on a train with reinforcements that Batista had sent from Havana. Once the rebels had derailed the train, the soldiers surrendered in droves. The **revolutionaries** had won the war.

◀ *Guevara gives an order to one of his soldiers during the Battle of Santa Clara.*

29

Once in Havana, Castro put Guevara in command of La Cabaña fortress, which had served the Batista **regime** as a barracks, weapons warehouse, and prison. Castro gave Guevara the job of rounding up Batista supporters who were responsible for war crimes. After the Battle of Santa Clara, Guevara had ordered the execution of several torturers. In the months following the end of fighting, the **revolutionaries** discovered many graves containing the bodies of Batista's victims. The revolutionaries tried a number of those responsible for the murders and sentenced about 550 people to death. The trials were probably less than fair, but the vast majority of the Cuban people supported the executions. Many wealthy Cubans had supported and benefited from the Batista regime but were not guilty of specific crimes against the people. The revolutionaries allowed these people to leave Cuba, and most of them headed for the United States.

Guevara also had several personal matters with which to deal. Hilda arrived in Cuba with their three-year-old daughter Hildita only to discover that Guevara had fallen in love with Aleida. Hilda reluctantly agreed to give him a divorce. Guevara made an effort to establish a relationship with Hildita. In January 1959 people often saw Guevara and Hildita walking around La Cabaña fortress hand in hand.

◀ Fidel and Guevara review a military parade in Cuba in August 1960.

That same month, Guevara's mother, father, sisters, and younger brother arrived from Argentina to see him. He took them on a tour and showed them the places where key events of the **revolutionary** war had taken place. He told them he would not return to his career in medicine or to Argentina.

Making victory count

In mid-January, Guevara suffered a severe **asthma** attack, probably brought on by the stress of his work at La Cabaña and the difficulties of his family life. Doctors sent him to recover in a house by the sea at Tarará, some twelve miles (nineteen kilometers) from Havana. There, he took a leading part in a series of unofficial gatherings at which Cuba's new leaders discussed the future of their **revolution.** Guevara was always in favor of the most far-reaching policies. He supported greater equality in wages and more long-term economic planning by the government. He also supported government control of industries and services and **land reform,** which involved breaking up all the large estates.

The revolutionaries had brought down Batista's government, Guevara argued, but how would they improve the lives of ordinary Cubans? They could do this only if they also destroyed the patterns of ownership and control (who owned what and who ran what) that Batista had supported and that rich Cubans and the United States still supported. Such a program would face great opposition, both inside and outside Cuba. The new Cuba, therefore, needed an efficient **security police** to reduce opposition to the new regime. The country also needed an army that was completely loyal to the new government. Furthermore, the country required complete **agrarian reform,** partly because the ordinary people needed more land and partly because the few rich people who owned most of the land had supported Batista. Taking land away from the rich would reduce their power to oppose the revolution.

In Guevara's view, the country also had to rely less on sugar production, which accounted for 40 percent of the national income and 80 percent of its exports. Cuba, he said, should create industries in the towns and grow a much wider variety of crops in the countryside.

Guevara was not a member of the **Communist** Party, but he considered himself a Communist. Believing, as he did, that the July 26 Movement and the Cuban Communist Party had similar goals, he encouraged them to work together. He also hoped that Cuba would become closer to the Soviet Union. The first **agrarian reform,** in May 1959, took large sugar and rice plantations away from U.S. companies and rich Cubans. This action met with stern opposition from the United States, which considered the repayment given for the land to be far too low. Though the reform was overwhelmingly popular in Cuba, the reactions it sparked made it obvious that the country needed all the friends it could find. Guevara knew that sooner or later the Cuban **Revolution** would bring about the same type of U.S. invasion that had toppled President Jacob Arbenz in Guatemala.

Ambassador and banker

In June, only ten days after his marriage to Aleida, Guevara set out on a three-month world tour to gather support for the revolution. He visited many

◀ *Guevara and his second wife Aleida leave for their honeymoon in June 1959.*

countries—Egypt, Japan, Yugoslavia, India, Sri Lanka, Indonesia, Pakistan, Sudan, and Morocco—and talked with many leaders of the **developing world.** He gave an honest opinion to some leaders. When Egypt's president, Gamal Abdel Nasser,

told Guevara that only a few Egyptians had fled after its revolution, he replied that it must not have been much of a revolution. But his judgment of other leaders showed his lack of experience. In Indonesia, for example, President Sukarno fooled him. Guevara mistook the corrupt **dictator** for a model leader in the developing world. Seeing what he wanted to see was one of Guevara's greatest weaknesses.

▲ *Guevara, the roving ambassador, meets with Egypt's president Nasser in July 1959.*

FOR DETAILS ON KEY PEOPLE OF GUEVARA'S TIME, SEE PAGE 58.

Before leaving Cuba, Castro had put Guevara in charge of the Industrial Department of the National Institute of Agrarian Reform (INRA). On his return, in September 1959, he resumed his work supervising reform of Cuba's important sugar industry. A few weeks later, Castro also appointed Guevara director of the National Bank, which put him in charge of the currency and Cuba's finances. Castro knew that Guevara had no great knowledge of economics, but he trusted him more than many of those who had. He also had great faith in Guevara's organizational skills. Fourteen months later, Guevara left the bank to become Minister of Industry, another key economic job. For about four years, from mid-1959 to mid-1963, Guevara ran Cuba's economy.

Guevara brought enthusiasm and what seemed like endless
energy to his work. He did his best to learn economics.
Perhaps most importantly, he brought a sense of discipline and
organizational ability to the early years of the Cuban
Revolution. To some, Guevara gave the impression that he
spent most of his time at the bank with his feet up on the
desk, chatting with friends. But he got the work done and
made sure that others did, too. He signed Cuban banknotes
"Che," which some people found casual and almost
disrespectful. But Guevara was making the point—that bank
presidents were no more important than sugarcane cutters
or mechanics.

A life of work

Guevara's official jobs were only part of the story. In
November 1959, he helped start the Volunteer Work Program.
This program put citizens to work evenings and weekends on
projects such as building schools, cutting sugarcane, or
performing other useful jobs. Such volunteer work made
people aware of how important it was to help one another
and strengthened their sense of community. Guevara
understood the importance of setting an example for the
people and happily gave up most of his Saturdays to
participate in the program.

Guevara also had to attend to government affairs, give
speeches, and have talks with the many foreigners who came
to Cuba eager to learn about the revolution. Guevara spent
many evenings writing *Guerrilla Warfare,* a manual for
revolutionary groups that he hoped would follow in Cuba's
footsteps. All this work left little time for family life. He and
Aleida lived in a comfortable, but small and modest house in
Havana's Nevado Vedado quarter. Though the two were

different in many ways, they were still in love. Late in 1960, they had their first child. They named her Aleidita—after Aleida's mother. Guevara's former wife Hilda had also settled in Havana, and his daughter Hildita usually stayed with her father on weekends.

Guevara could have filled his home with the gifts given to him on his foreign trips, but he gave all of them away to youth training centers. Neither would he let Aleida take advantage of his position. When she wanted to take the children to school in his government car, he insisted that she take the bus, "like everyone else."

◄ *Guevara sets an example by doing volunteer work in the early years of the revolution.*

The Bay of Pigs

By this time, the disputes between Cuba and the United States had snowballed into a full-scale crisis. In 1960, the United States first reduced the amount of Cuban sugar it was buying. Then it stopped buying it altogether, an act that threatened serious damage to Cuba's economy. Fortunately for Cuba, help was available. The **Cold War** conflict between the United States and the Soviet Union, which had become more dangerous in the late 1950s, meant that the Soviets were happy to help any enemies of the United States. They agreed to buy Cuba's sugar.

U.S.-Cuban relations worsened. When U.S.-owned oil refineries in Cuba refused to refine oil that Cuba had bought from the Soviet Union, the Cuban government seized the

refineries. The United States responded with an economic **embargo**—banning trade between Cuba and the United States in everything but food and medicine. The Cubans then took over 166 additional U.S. companies and built an even closer bond with the Soviet Union. In October 1960, Guevara led the first official Cuban mission to Moscow.

◀ *Castro and Guevara walk with Deputy Premier Anastas Mikoyan of the Soviet Union.*

Guevara's hope

"The only privileged people in Cuba will be the children."

(Guevara, quoted in 1961, claiming that
children would be put first in the new Cuba)

The U.S. government financed and supported antirevolutionary Cuban **exiles** (people who had fled to the United States from Cuba when the Batista regime fell). Throughout the year, the exiles carried on a campaign of **sabotage** and **terrorism** against the island. It seemed only a matter of time before the United States invaded Cuba. Finally, in April 1961, an army of 1,500 exiles, supported by U.S. planes, landed at Playa Giron, or the Bay of Pigs, on Cuba's southern shore. The Cuban army and its people, whom Castro had armed to defend the still-popular **revolution,** swiftly defeated the exile forces.

Placed in charge of the western portion of the island, Guevara was not involved in the fighting. However, he was wounded. He dropped a gun, which accidentally fired, and the bullet struck him in the cheek. Had he been holding the gun at a slightly different angle, the bullet would have killed him. Instead, he spent a day in the hospital and several more recovering from the injury.

The Bay of Pigs invasion gave Guevara some satisfaction because it had proved him right—the United States was indeed a determined enemy of the Cuban Revolution. The time had come to choose sides once and for all, and for Cuba to join the **Communist bloc.**

7 Falling Out with the Soviets

Cuba's victory at the Bay of Pigs offered proof of the continuing popularity of the **revolution** and its leader. But that popularity was about to be tested to the limit. The Cuban economy, for which Guevara was responsible, was heading into a nosedive. Goods were in short supply, and early in 1962 the government introduced **rationing** for a long list of basic items, including rice, beans, eggs, milk, toothpaste, and detergent. What had gone wrong?

Reasons for economic failure

The dispute with the United States had partly caused the collapse of the Cuban economy. Before the revolution, the United States had been Cuba's most important trade partner. Cuba had bought nearly everything it needed from the United States and had sold almost everything it produced to its northern neighbor. Now, Cuba had to find new markets. It also had to find a source of spare parts for all the U.S. goods and machines that Cuba had bought in the past.

Not everything could be blamed on the U.S. **embargo,** however. The Cubans and Guevara had made serious mistakes of their own. For example, they had spent too much money on huge increases in health care and education for ordinary people. Cuba needed better health care and education—they were what the revolution was all about—but the country could not afford them.

In addition, Castro's attempt to reduce Cuba's dependence on sugar by growing other crops and creating new industries went badly wrong. The program had been poorly planned and tried to do too much too soon. The sugar harvest had certainly been reduced, but the money lost in sugar sales had not been made up in other ways. As a result, the government had less to spend on the raw materials it needed for the new industries. Clearly, the Cubans were beginners when it came to planning an economy.

They hoped for help from the Soviet Union, both in knowledge and equipment. But the quality of help they received was much poorer, and the price much higher, than they had expected. To make matters even worse, the Cubans soon realized that the Soviets expected more than money in return for their aid. The Soviets also demanded a say in how Cuba used the aid. Between 1961 and 1964, Guevara's work in Cuba was greatly influenced by his growing disappointment in the Soviets.

▼ *In New York, Cuban* **exiles** *demonstrate against the Castro* **regime.** *Many wealthy landowners, business leaders, scientists, engineers, teachers, doctors, artists, and writers fled to the United States in the 1950s. Their departure damaged the Cuban economy.*

Two ways forward

Gradually, Guevara realized that a basic choice faced Cuba—
to run the country the Soviet way or his way. As far as Cuba
was concerned, the Soviet way meant relying on sugar by
producing and selling as much of it as it could to other
Communist countries and using the earnings to pay for
clinics and schools and a few new industries.

In return for its guarantee to buy all the sugar Cuba could
produce, the Soviet Union demanded something in return—
political loyalty. The Cubans would be required to organize
their society according to the Soviet model. The Soviets
wanted Cuba to introduce economic reforms similar to those

Soviet leader Nikita Khrushchev makes a point at a press conference
in 1959.

that the Soviet leader, Nikita Khrushchev, and his successors were introducing. Under these reforms, the government would reward the best-run farms and businesses, and the most valuable workers would receive higher wages. The Soviets also expected Cuba to support the Soviet policy of **peaceful coexistence** with the United States. Cuba was not to offer help to other armed revolutions anywhere else.

FOR DETAILS ON KEY PEOPLE OF GUEVARA'S TIME, SEE PAGE **58.**

Guevara had different ideas. He thought the Soviets should be more generous in their dealings with developing countries such as Cuba. They should not, he believed, treat such countries as a **capitalist** country would, by demanding the highest prices for their goods. More importantly, Guevara was growing more and more opposed to Soviet policies, both at home and abroad. For Guevara, paying people more for working harder was a betrayal of **Communism.** He wanted to pay all workers the same wages and to rely on enthusiasm and willpower to get them to work harder.

Such a program, he believed, would create the conditions for both economic and political success. After all, **socialism** and Communism were about more than raising the material standing of living. These systems also wanted to create a new type of individual who was motivated by love of other human beings and a sense of duty, rather than by greed.

A lost battle

In the fall of 1962, the Cuban Missile Crisis erupted. Although it had no real affect on the economic and political future of the Cuban **Revolution,** it certainly increased Guevara's disillusionment with the Soviet Union. Until then, he had favored placing Soviet missiles in Cuba—"anything that can stop the Americans is worthwhile," he had said.

▲ *President John F. Kennedy (center) meets with U.S. army officials during the Cuban Missile Crisis of 1962.*

Guevara was furious when Khrushchev, under intense pressure from U.S. president John F. Kennedy, agreed to remove the missiles. Guevara's anger helps to explain some of his more extreme statements at this time. For example, he claimed that the Cuban people were "prepared to be atomically incinerated so that their ashes may be used as the foundations of new societies." Guevara was assuming that everyone else would make the same sacrifices as he would. As it turned out, Guevara was wrong.

The Soviets also infuriated Castro, but he knew that in the end Cuba depended on Soviet help and good will. In economic matters, his heart agreed with Guevara, but his head told him that the Soviet way was the only practical solution. In the spring of 1963, Castro spent more than a month in the Soviet Union, trying to get the best deal for Cuba. In January 1964, the two countries signed a long-term agreement. Cuba would limit its economic activities to the production of sugar and other agricultural products for sale in the Soviet Union and

The Cuban Missile Crisis

In 1962, after the Bay of Pigs invasion, the Soviet Union supplied Cuba with nuclear missiles. The United States objected to the installation of these missiles so close to its shores. It imposed a **naval blockade** around Cuba to prevent the delivery of any more missiles and demanded that the Soviets withdraw those that they had already placed there. Threatened with the possibility of a nuclear war, the Soviets, without consulting the Cubans, agreed to withdraw the missiles. In return, the United States promised not to invade Cuba and to remove its own nuclear warheads from Turkey.

Eastern Europe and would receive industrial goods in return. The Cuban **Communists** would have to do what the Soviets told them to do. Guevara had lost his battle for a different way of building Communism in Cuba, and he knew it.

Time to leave?

Guevara continued to write articles and give speeches around the world, hoping to inspire both present and future generations with his vision and determination. Yet, in 1964 his thoughts turned away from the battle he had lost in Cuba and toward the battles that he might win elsewhere in the world.

Key dates in the Cuban Revolution

1956	• November	*Granma* sails for Cuba
1959	• January	Victorious army of the July 26 Movement enters Havana
1959–1960		Series of increasingly bitter disputes flare between Cuba and the United States
1961	• April	U.S.-supported invasion of Cuba lands in the Bay of Pigs
1962	• October	Cuban Missile Crisis
1963–1964		Cuba's economic ties with the Soviet Union are strengthened
1965	• April	Guevara leaves Cuba after giving up all his official jobs

8 Failure in Africa

A tough decision now faced Guevara. It was hard to think about leaving Castro, whom he still loved and respected despite their differences. He said at this point that he found it difficult to imagine either marriage or divorce where Castro was concerned. In other words, he could neither stay with his old friend nor leave him. He also had to consider his family. He and Aleida now had three children: Aleidita, their first son Camilo born in May 1962, and their second daughter Celia born in June 1963. And Guevara was still immensely popular among the Cuban people. They had taken the Argentinian to their hearts and kept him there, despite the economic failures. Yet, in the end he had to go.

Where should Guevara go to start a new **revolution? Latin America** naturally drew him, but he had good reasons for looking elsewhere. For one thing, the United States was likely to take Cuban interference in Latin America seriously. For another, most Latin American **Communist** parties obediently followed the Soviet idea that power should be won politically rather than through **guerrilla** warfare. If Guevara did start such a war somewhere in Latin America, then the Soviets would probably ensure that he would receive little help from the cities—where most Communist Party members lived.

Choosing Congo

Wanting to find somewhere outside U.S. and Soviet influence, Guevara looked to Africa. Touring the continent in December 1964 and January 1965, he met with leaders of countries that had recently won independence from the old **colonial** powers. He also saw as much as he could of the lives of Africa's ordinary people. The poverty and **oppression** he saw there moved him and persuaded him that he could do something about it. Congo, in particular, caught his attention.

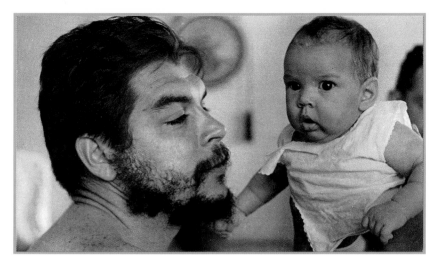

▲ *Guevara holds his first-born son Camilo.*

FOR DETAILS ON KEY PEOPLE OF GUEVARA'S TIME, SEE PAGE 58.

A revolution seemed to be already underway in this huge country at the heart of Africa. If successful, it might spill across its borders and set the whole continent ablaze.

Back in Cuba, Guevara persuaded Castro to allow him to lead a small force of Cuban soldiers to Congo. Aleida had just given birth to the couple's second son Ernesto (born on February 24, 1965) and was upset at his leaving. However, this second marriage, like the first, was less important to Guevara than his personal mission. If he did not come back, he told her, she should remarry.

Problems, problems

Guevara arrived in Tanzania in mid-April 1965 with the first of the 130 Cubans selected for the expedition. Almost all of them were Afro-Cubans, since Guevara felt that Africans might not trust white Cubans. A few days later, Guevara and his soldiers crossed Lake Tanganyika and set up camp in the village of Kibamba on the Congolese side. The Congolese rebels under Laurent Kabila controlled this territory. They were fighting to overthrow the pro-Western government of Moise Tshombe. Kibamba would be Guevara's headquarters for seven frustrating months.

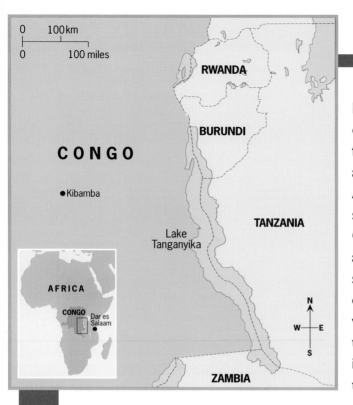

▲ *This map shows where Guevara and his small group of revolutionaries tried to start a revolution in Congo.*

In Congo, Guevara was in charge of his small Cuban force, but he had no authority over anyone else. At the beginning, this seemed only right. It was a Congolese **revolution,** he argued, and the Congolese should be giving the military orders. He and his Cubans were there to help train the locals, to support them in action if necessary, but not to do their fighting for them.

However, Kabila and the other Congolese leaders understood the situation better than Guevara. They knew that the revolution had little chance of success and preferred to live comfortably in exile rather than organize any fighting. Left to fend for themselves in the camps, Congolese troops drank, fought among themselves, and bullied the local **peasants.** They explained to their astonished Cuban trainers that *dawa* protected them. It was the power of a potion that, once rubbed over their bodies, would protect them from bullets.

Guevara also had personal problems. The climate was terrible for his **asthma,** and he suffered frequent attacks, losing almost a quarter of his body weight. At the end of May, he received news from Cuba that his mother was dying in Argentina. His family had tried to reach him earlier, but his presence in Africa was still supposed to be a secret.

His mother died without knowing why he had not come to her or sent word.

Defeat

When Kabila finally ordered his forces to attack a government stronghold, it was a disaster. Many of the Congolese troops ran away the moment they came under fire, and opposing forces killed four of the Cubans accompanying them. That battle revealed that Cuban fighters were in Africa. As a result, the Congolese government ordered its powerful army of white **mercenaries** to drive them out. Guevara's troops enjoyed one successful ambush in July, but their situation quickly grew worse during the next few months.

In November, a change in the Congolese government persuaded Tanzania and other African countries to end their support for the rebellion. Without this support, Guevara and his men could not continue. They withdrew across the lake to Tanzania, and Guevara's men returned to Cuba. Weak and discouraged, Guevara spent several months recovering his strength, first in the Tanzanian capital of Dar es Salaam and then in Prague, the capital of **Communist** Czechoslovakia. What should he do now?

Congo

During its first five years of independence (1960–1965) the former Belgian Congo witnessed the murder of one prime minister, Patrice Lumumba, and a failed attempt by the country's richest province Katanga to gain independence. It also saw the arrival and departure of a United Nations peacekeeping force and armed uprisings in many different parts of the country. Congo seemed, in many ways, ripe for revolution. However, by the time Guevara arrived in the spring of 1965, the government, with the help of white mercenaries, had stopped most of the rebellious activity. Guevara was, as the Algerian leader, Ben Bella, said, "too late."

Following his defeat in Africa, Guevara's first instinct was to make Argentina his next target. Castro believed that this would be little more than a suicide mission and tried to persuade Guevara that Bolivia was a better bet. In Bolivia, Castro and others argued, the countryside was better suited to **guerrilla warfare.** Bolivia had a strong **left-wing** tradition and recruits for the **guerrilla** army would be easier to find. Like Congo, Bolivia sat in the center of a huge land mass and could be used as a base for **revolutionary** action in many other countries, including, in the long run, Argentina.

Beaten before he began

Guevara allowed himself to be persuaded, and in July 1966 he returned to Cuba for the last time. During the next three months, he selected and prepared the team of Cubans and

▼ *Surrounded by local people, Guevara (seated, on the right) studies a map during the final weeks of his war in Bolivia.*

Saying his good-byes

In October 1966, Guevara said good-bye to Aleida and to their four children. Disguised as an old man for his trip to Bolivia—with his hair plucked out to make him appear bald and dressed in a suit, tie, and glasses—he introduced himself to the children as their "Uncle Ramon" and told them how much their father loved them.

At the training camp, Guevara and Castro, sitting side by side on a log, shared a long farewell conversation. Castro tried to talk Guevara into postponing the operation, but he refused. They hugged each other and then sat together for a long time in silence.

Bolivians that would fight under him in Bolivia. He lived at a mountain training camp. Aleida often came to visit him.

Late in October 1966, Guevara traveled to Bolivia. Two possible locations had been suggested for a guerrilla base. Under pressure from the Bolivian **Communist** Party and its leader, Mario Monje, Guevara selected Ñancahuazú, the location closest to Argentina. The other location offered better cover for guerrilla activity and more people from which to draw recruits. But the Bolivian Communist Party wanted to steer Guevara away from its own territory.

Upon reaching Ñancahuazú, Guevara had good reason to be depressed. Only a few men waited for him, and weapons, medicine, and food were in short supply. In December, Monje arrived at the camp to demand the final say in any action proposed by Guevara and his soldiers. Guevara, remembering what had happened in Africa, refused to surrender his leadership.

From this point on, Monje and the Bolivian Communist Party did more harm than good. They worked to prevent Bolivians from joining the **guerrillas.** Guevara's army consisted of only about 30 fighters, and it would never grow much bigger.

Slide to disaster

In February 1967, Guevara led his men on a mission to explore the local area. It was supposed to last two weeks, but it took six. The thorny vegetation ripped the men's clothes and boots to shreds, serious insect bites covered their skin, and two men drowned in swollen rivers. Hungry and thirsty, Guevara's soldiers bickered angrily. They were near **mutiny** before they had even faced a human enemy.

The men returned to Ñancahuazú to find that the Bolivian army had discovered their base and waited for their return. Guevara managed to successfully ambush the army unit, but he probably should have just walked away. Now the authorities were certain that Guevara's troops posed a real threat. The guerrillas had no hope of recruiting new fighters, creating a network of supporters in the city, or talking to the outside world. They were on their own.

Guevara split his force in two, hoping to join them again at a later date. But the two columns never saw each other again. Hunted by the Bolivian army, the two columns marched around the area looking for each other. They stopped to occupy an occasional village, but they never felt strong enough to attack a military target. Neither the local peasants nor the cities helped them. Even Cuba abandoned them because it did not want to anger the Soviets. They had warned Castro that they would cut off economic aid to Cuba if he went against their policy of not supporting armed struggles.

The end

Weakened by **asthma** attacks and stomach problems, Guevara struggled on. At the end of August, the Bolivians ambushed the second column of soldiers crossing a river and killed most of its members. In early October, the Bolivians finally trapped Guevara's own column in the Yuro Ravine.

Wounded in the leg and unable to walk, the Bolivians took Guevara prisoner. His captors held him in the schoolhouse of La Higuera, a nearby town. Not knowing what to do with him, his captors asked their superiors for instructions. The following morning, October 9, 1967, orders arrived from the capital. Their superiors told them to put Guevara to death. The soldiers guarding him drew lots, and the man selected to perform the execution shot Guevara as he lay helpless on the floor of the schoolhouse.

▼ *Members of the Bolivian armed forces display Guevara's dead body in the hospital morgue at Vallegrande.*

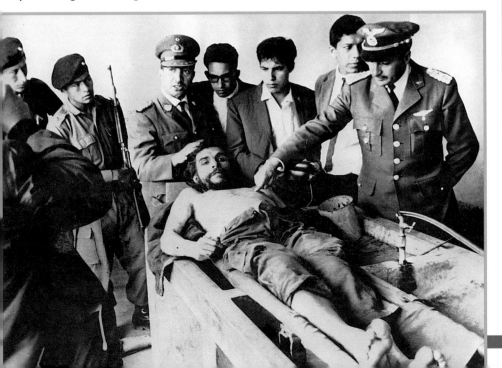

51

Guevara once told his children that he hoped **imperialism**—the exploitation of poor countries by richer ones—would be gone by the end of the 1900s. In this, as in so much else, his dreams would not come true. More than 30 years have passed since Guevara's death, and the system he fought seems as strong as ever. The gap between rich and poor has, if anything, grown wider. Solutions to the social and political injustices he saw in **Latin America** and Africa are as hard to come up with now as they were then.

The style of **guerrilla warfare** Guevara practiced, wrote about, and supported has proved a costly failure in many places where groups have tried it. The kind of **Communism** Guevara came to despise in the Soviet Union has all but vanished. In addition, the type of Communism he

◀ *This statue of Guevara holding a child is in Santa Clara, Cuba.*

hoped to build in Cuba and elsewhere has not worked out either. Guevara's beloved Cuban **Revolution** is no longer the inspiration it once was.

Successes and failures

Guevara's contributions to the success of the Cuban **revolutionary** war were huge. His physical courage, intelligence, and vision shaped Cuban Communism in its early years. As long as Guevara had any say in the matter, Communists always kept their promises to the Cuban people and never surrendered to the revolution's enemies.

In his work, personal style, and writings, Guevara gave the Cuban Revolution a romantic appeal that reached far beyond Cuba. He was a **Communist,** but one who seemed different from those in power elsewhere. Unlike them, he spoke his mind and seemed driven, not by personal gain, but by a genuine desire to build a better, fairer world.

When Guevara failed, it was usually because he was attempting the impossible. He spent his life fighting the crippling disease of **asthma.** His refusal to accept his own weaknesses, in this and other matters, was reckless. But it was also heroic. However, because he often refused to accept the shortcomings of others, he sometimes treated people with cruelty, as he himself admitted. Guevara's major failures—with the Cuban economy, and in Africa and Bolivia—had a lot to do with his inability to see people as they really were instead of how he believed they should be.

The way to Communism

Guevara's most important legacy is probably his contribution to **socialist** and **Communist** thought. The story of the 1900s was largely the story of **Communism**'s rise and fall, and Guevara's own story was a part of this. His faith in Soviet Communism went away once he learned how it really worked. In his final years, he talked and wrote a great deal about creating a better, more human form of Communism.

▼ *Thousands wave flags and display portraits of Guevara during his official funeral on October 17, 1997, almost 30 years after his death.*

Like two other leading figures of the 1900s, Mohandas Gandhi and Martin Luther King Jr., Guevara realized that the way in which you go about getting something affects what you get. Just as Gandhi and King believed that social harmony could never be achieved through violence, so Guevara believed that

Communism could never be created with **capitalist** methods. If a government appealed only to the greedy—as he believed the Soviet government did in the 1960s—it would never create a society in which people cared for one another. Communism, Guevara believed, first had to find a place in people's hearts. If it did that, then the social benefits would follow.

Self-sacrifice

Finally, and most obviously, Guevara's life and death have come to represent an example to others. As he saw it, the point of life was to help those less fortunate, and he lived accordingly. However, Guevara's following of his own ideals was hard for those closest to him.

Some people believe that the world today is too concerned with personal pleasure and getting rich. When viewed this way, it is hard to find fault with someone, like Guevara, whose life was driven by hatred of injustice. As Guevara himself wrote in his last letter to his family: "Many will call me an adventurer, and I am, but of a different kind—one who risks his skin to prove his convictions."

The legend

"For millions of the dispossessed [people who have been denied the basic necessities of life] all over Latin America, there were no other heroes. Che was a necessity, not a possibility; if he had not existed, they would have invented him anyway, and often did. The point of the legend was always the same, and as powerful as it was simple: Che lived and died for us."

(Author Patrick Symmes from his book *Chasing Che*)

Timeline

1928	Born in Rosario, Argentina, on May 14
1930	First asthma attack
1932	Family moves to Alta Gracia, Argentina
1936–1939	Spanish Civil War
1939–1945	World War II
1948	Enters the university to study medicine
1952	Travels throughout South America with Alberto Granado
1953	Arrives in Guatemala
1954	Meets Hilda Gadea and Cuban exiles U.S.-supported invasion of Guatemala Travels in Mexico
1955	Meets Fidel Castro and agrees to join his revolutionary group Marries Hilda
1956	First daughter Hilda Beatriz Guevara (Hildita) born Sets sail with Castro in the *Granma* Castro's force almost destroyed in Battle of Alegría de Pío
1957	Promoted to *Comandante*, given command of Second Column
1958	Leads column from Sierra Maestra to the center of the island Meets Aleida Cuban forces win the Battle of Santa Clara

1959	Takes over command of La Cabaña fortress
	Asks Hilda for divorce
	Agrarian Reform Bill denounced by United States
	Marries Aleida
	Becomes head of the National Bank

1960	U.S.-owned refineries refuse to handle Soviet oil
	U.S. government suspends Cuba's right to sell sugar in United States
	United States imposes trade embargo on Cuba
	Second daughter Aleidita born

| 1961 | Becomes Minister of Industry |
| | U.S.-supported invasion of Cuba defeated at Playa Giron (Bay of Pigs) |

| 1961–1963 | Cuban economy in steep decline |

| 1962 | First son Camilo born |
| | Cuban Missile Crisis |

| 1963 | Third daughter Celia born |

| 1963 | Cuba forms closer links with the Soviet Union and follows Soviet economic policies |

| 1964 | Castro agrees to economic deal with the Soviets |

1965	Second son Ernesto born
	Arrives in Tanzania and travels to Congo
	Mother dies in Argentina

| 1966 | Last time in Cuba, says good-bye to his children |
| | Meeting with Bolivian Communist leader, Monje |

1967	Six-week reconnaissance march
	Group discovered by Bolivian army
	Captured and murdered by the Bolivian army

| 1997 | Remains found and returned to Cuba for official funeral |

Key People of Guevara's Time

Fulgencio Batista (1901–1973) The son of a Cuban laborer, Batista rose to power as the leader of an army revolt in 1933 and ruled Cuba as a **dictator** until 1940, when Cuba elected him president. During this first period in power, he introduced some much-needed reform but was defeated in an election in 1944. His second **dictatorship,** which began with another military coup in 1952, was notorious for its corruption and brutality. Fidel Castro's July 26 Movement finally overthrew him early in 1959.

Fidel Castro (1927–) The son of a sugarcane farmer, Castro studied and practiced law in Cuba's capital of Havana in the early 1950s. In July 1953, he led an unsuccessful attack on the Moncada barracks in Santiago de Cuba. The government sentenced him to fifteen years in prison. Released after two years, he formed the July 26 Movement (named after the date of the attack) and planned and executed a sea invasion of Cuba from Mexico. Once established in the Sierra Maestra, Castro led a successful civil war against the Batista dictatorship, entering Havana in triumph in January 1959. During the early years of the **revolution,** U.S. hostility toward Castro's policies and aims forced him to form a relationship with the Soviet Union, which lasted until the collapse of that country in 1991. Castro's regime survived the fall of **Communism** in Europe, and he remains a powerful influence, both in Cuba and on the world stage.

Laurent Kabila (1938–2001) Kabila was the leader of the rebels in the area of Congo chosen by Guevara for the Cuban support force. Kabila's unwillingness to assume any direct responsibility for military action was one of the main reasons for Guevara's frustration in Africa. Kabila led the mixed Congolese-Rwandan forces that overthrew Congo's president Mobutu Sese Seko in 1997. However, once in power he showed little interest in improving the conditions of the Congolese people. One of his own bodyguards assassinated him in 2001 for reasons that remain a mystery.

John F. Kennedy (1917–1963) Kennedy took office as president of the United States in January 1960. Throughout his election campaign, he insisted that something be done about Cuba. By this time, plans for the Bay of Pigs invasion of Cuba were well underway, and Kennedy decided to follow through with the plans. When the invasion failed, he ordered a campaign of disruption and **sabotage** (Operation Mongoose) against the island. On discovering, in the summer of 1962, that the Soviets had installed missiles in Cuba, he risked nuclear war to force their withdrawal. Lee Harvey Oswald assassinated him in Dallas, Texas, on November 22, 1963.

Nikita Khrushchev (1894–1971) Elected first secretary of the Soviet Communist Party in 1953, Khrushchev quickly became the undisputed leader of the Soviet Union. He was in charge during the Cuban Revolution and the growth of his country's economic and political ties with Cuba. He also played a key role in the Cuban Missile Crisis. Failures at home and abroad led to his removal from office in 1964.

Ahmed Ben Bella (1916–) Bella became the first prime minister and president of Algeria following his country's successful war of independence against the French. When neighboring Morocco threatened Algeria, the Cubans offered military support, and Bella had the first of many meetings with Guevara. The two men became friends, and Guevara relied on Bella's knowledge of African affairs when it came to planning his own intervention in the Congo.

Sources for Further Research

Blackthorn, John. *I, Che Guevara: A Novel*. New York: William Morrow and Company, 2000.

Connolly, Sean. *Heinemann Profiles: Fidel Castro*. Chicago: Heinemann Library, 2001.

Frost, Helen. *A Look at Cuba*. Minnetonka, Minn.: Capstone Press, 2002.

Gee, Martha B. ed. *A Child's Glimpse of Cuba*. New York: Friendship Press, 1999.

Gibb, Tom. *Fidel Castro: Leader of Cuba's Revolution*. Chicago: Raintree, 2001.

Guevara, Ernesto "Che." *Che Guevara Talks to Young People*. New York: Pathfinder Press, 2000.

Guevara, Ernesto "Che." *The Motorcycle Diaries*. New York: Verso, 1996.

Leonard, Thomas M. *Castro and the Cuban Revolution*. Westport, Conn.: Greenwood Publishing, 1999.

Ryan, Henry B. *The Fall of Che Guevara: A Story of Soldiers, Spies, and Diplomats*. New York: Oxford University Press, 1999.

Glossary

adrenaline naturally-occurring substance in the body that can be used to ease an asthma attack

agrarian reform see **land reform**

allergies harmful reactions to certain substances, such as foods, pollen, and dust

Amazon basin the huge area, mostly in Brazil, watered by the Amazon River

amnesty general pardon granted to offenders

Andean people Native Americans living in the Andes Mountains

asthma disease in which the tightening of muscles in the tubes connecting the throat with the lungs causes difficulty in breathing

asylum a place of safety. The word is also often used to describe places where the mentally or physically ill have been kept separate from the rest of society.

capitalism economic system in which the production and distribution of goods depend on private wealth and profit-making

Cold War name given to the hostility that existed between the capitalist West and Communist East between 1947 and the late 1980s

colonial having to do with colonies, or the system by which they were ruled. The term usually refers to the period of European colonialism, between the 1400s and the mid-1900s.

Communism an economic system in which property is held by the government rather than by individuals. The term is usually associated with governments that give little freedom to their people and a system of economic planning that was created in the Soviet Union during the 1920s and 1930s.

Communist someone who supports Communism, or having to do with Communism

Communist bloc group of Communist countries led by the Soviet Union. The bloc included all the Eastern European Communist nations except Yugoslavia and the Asian countries of North Vietnam, North Korea, and, until the early 1960s, China.

courier person who carries messages

cremated burned after death

democratically elected chosen for political office by a free vote of the adult population

developing world poorer countries of the world, which include many countries in Africa, Asia, and Latin America

dictator person who rules on his or her own, without necessarily taking into account the wishes of the people

dictatorship government by an individual (called a dictator) or a small group that does not allow the people any say in their government

elite in politics, a small group of people that holds most of the political or economic power or both

embargo policy of not buying from or selling to a particular nation

exiles people who live outside their own country, whether by choice or because they have been forced to leave

guerrilla member of a small armed band usually formed to fight against either an occupying force or an undemocratic government

guerrilla warfare war fought by unofficial, nongovernment troops, often in a rugged countryside

immigrant someone who settles in a foreign land after leaving his or her own country

imperialism until the mid-1900s, the open political and military domination of weaker countries by more powerful ones. Since the mid-1900s, the economic domination of weaker countries by more powerful ones.

Inca Native American people that established a large empire around 1200 C.E. in the Andes Mountains of present-day Peru, Bolivia, and Ecuador. The Spanish destroyed the Inca Empire in the 1530s.

indigenous native to, or belonging in, a particular place

land reform changing the pattern of land ownership. Over the last 100 years, land reform has usually involved breaking up large estates owned by wealthy individuals and turning the land over to farmers who have little or no land of their own.

Latin America those areas of the Western Hemisphere that include Spanish-speaking South and Central America, the Spanish-speaking Caribbean islands, and Portuguese-speaking Brazil.

left-wing in politics, a word to describe policies that place the needs of the whole community above the short-term wants or needs of the individual. Traditionally, socialism represents a moderate version of left-wing thought, and Communism represents a more extreme version.

leper colony traditionally, an area reserved for people suffering from leprosy, designed to separate them from the rest of the community

leprosy infectious disease of the skin and nerve-endings

mercenaries soldiers fighting in a country other than their own with the sole aim of earning money

mutiny open revolt by soldiers of lower ranks against their superior officers

naval blockade use of ships to prevent other ships from reaching a particular destination or country

nobility people who have inherited their membership in the ruling elite from their ancestors

oppression harsh rule

peaceful coexistence name given by the Soviet leaders to their policy of peaceful economic competition with the United States. The Soviets' belief was that once they had proved that Communism was economically more successful than capitalism, then there would no longer be any need for violent revolutions.

peasant poor farm worker

philosophy study of the causes and nature of human existence

puma another name for a cougar

radical in politics, supporting far-reaching changes in a government

rationing system of fairly dividing up goods that are in short supply

regime in politics, a government and its supporting organizations

revolution in politics, the overthrowing of the existing order in its entirety, not merely the replacement of one group of leaders by another

revolutionary someone committed to supporting and fighting for revolutions

sabotage deliberate damage

security police police force concerned with the security of the nation

skirmish brief battle, usually between small groups of soldiers

socialism set of political ideas that puts more importance on the needs of the community as a whole and less on the short-term wants or needs of the individual

socialist someone who believes in socialism

Spanish Civil War (1936–1939) war between Spain's liberal, democratically elected government and right-wing rebels, called Nationalists. The Nationalists won the war and set up a dictatorship under Francisco Franco that lasted until his death in 1975.

terrorism use of violence against civilian populations—either by states, groups, or individuals—with the intention of spreading fear or terror

Index